KINGDOM

&

COVENANT

A tale of two cities, two covenants,

And two kingdoms

" And we know that all things work together for good to them that love God, to them who are the called according to his purpose."

Romans 8:28

KINGDOM

&

COVENANT

A tale of two cities, two covenants,

And two kingdoms

ELDER DORIAN G. NEWTON

KNOWCHRISTTODAY.ORG
PUBLISHERS, L.L.C.
Chesapeake, VA 23320
www.KnowChristToday.org

KINGDOM & COVENANT:

A TALE OF TWO CITIES, TWO COVENANTS, AND TWO KINGDOMS

ISBN 13: 978-0-615-55965-0

ISBN 10: 0-615-55965-4

Published by

KNOWCHRISTTODAY.ORG
PUBLISHERS, L.L.C.
Chesapeake, VA 23320
www.KnowChristToday.org

Dedication

This study is dedicated to those who do not yet know Jesus Christ as their personal Lord and Savior. For those of you who don't know Him, I pray for seeds to be planted in your lives from this study which will spring up and *"and bare fruit an hundredfold."* **Luke 8:8**

Contents

Foreword by Dr. Minnie B. Washington 9

Preface 11

What We Believe................................13

Let's Begin...................................19

Bible Studies easy as 1, 2, 3...................21

Leading this as a small group Bible study?........25

Introduction 27

Our Condition................................29

God's Response 33

Defining The Kingdom........................41

Week 1: What is a Kingdom?..................45

Week 2: Kingdom Purpose & Provision..........53

Week 3: Kingdom Promise.....................57

A Tale of Two Cities........................67

Week 4: Babylon 69

Week 5: Jerusalem 75

Week 6: From Babel to Pentecost 81

Covenant Defined 87

Week 7: Blood Covered...91

Week 8: Blood Connected...95

Week 9: Blood Committed 105

The Promises of God 113

Week 10: Abraham's Covenant 115

Week 11: The Land (Moses' Covenant)...............127

Week 12: The Seed (David's Covenant) 133

Week 13: The Blessing (New Covenant)..............143

Week 14: "All the promises of God in Him are yes!" 149

Conclusion 161

FOREWORD

BY DR. MINNIE B. WASHINGTON

I have known Elder Dorian Gregory Newton for seventeen years and have been his pastor/overseer for the past four years; therefore, I know him personally and endorse his ministry.

The inspired writings of Dorian are divinely anointed by God for such a time as this. I believe it is of utmost importance to widely disseminate the teachings that God has given to him. God has truly placed His approval on Dorian's work by anointing his ministry and will give this message a wide acceptance. Therefore, I pray that its wide distribution will be the cause of many souls coming to know the Lord and making preparations to spend eternity in heaven.

KINGDOM AND COVENANT is the result of much prayer and hard work. Therefore, as you study this book, you'll be enlightened and brought to a new level of understanding concerning "Kingdom" and "Covenant." Although it is a careful process, as you study, you will gain a better understanding of how the Old Testament relates to the New Testament on this topic. More importantly, you'll profit in general by becoming more aware of and knowledgeable in your spirit concerning the things of God.

In closing, I pray that you will study these lessons through "opened" eyes unveiled by the Holy Spirit. I challenge you to study every chapter prayerfully and intently. Allow your mind to open up, because the truths shared with you are beyond milk and meat.

PREFACE

KnowChristToday.org is a teaching ministry founded *" for the perfecting of the saints, for the work of the ministry, for the edifying of the body of Christ..."* "That we henceforth be no more children, tossed to and fro, and carried about with every wind of doctrine, by the sleight of men, and cunning craftiness, whereby they lie in wait to deceive; but speaking the truth in love, may grow up into him in all things, which is the head, even Christ." **Ephesians 4:12, 14-15**

Our website provides leadership training, podcasts of sermons and lectures, various trainings and teaching ministries, a monthly e-newsletter, Bible study instruction and resource materials, access to published materials produced by the ministry and a calendar of local events and activities.

MISSION

To populate the Kingdom of God by equipping people who cannot be shaken and are always battle ready to face the world, walking in the power of the Holy Spirit with integrity and the personality of Jesus Christ for effective Christian living.

Acknowledgements

First giving honor to God; who is the head of my life and to my Lord and Savior Jesus Christ. I give honor to my pastor, to my bishop, and my to fellow laborers in Christ. I also give honor to my mother whose support and prayers continue to sustain me in my ministry.

I thank my Tabernacle of Prayer Church family, especially each of the students of the "Freedom in Redemption Evangelism" ministry, for your support and encouragement during the preparation of this study. I thank every family member, friend and co-worker for your prayers and support during this process. Last, but definitely not least, I thank and honor my wife, Jermaine, for her prayers, patience and support while I have spent long nights and countless hours working on this study.

Thank you all and God bless you.

Elder Dorian G. Newton

What We Believe

THE SCRIPTURES

We believe that <u>only</u> the sixty-six books of the Bible are the inspired, and therefore inerrant, Word of God. It is the final authority for all we believe and how we are to live. **Matthew 5:18; John 10:35; 17:17; 2 Timothy 3:16-17; 2 Peter 1:20-21**

THE GODHEAD

We believe that the one true God exists eternally in three persons, Father, Son, and Holy Spirit, who are equal in deity, power, and glory. We believe that God not only created the world but also now upholds, sustains, governs, and directs all that exists and that He will bring all things to their proper consummation in Christ Jesus to the glory of His name. **Psalm 104; Psalm 139; Matthew 10:29-31; 28:19; Acts 17:24-28; 2 Corinthians 13:14; Ephesians 1:9-12; 4:4-6; Colossians 1:16-17; Hebrews 1:1-3; Revelation 1:4-6**

THE LORD JESUS CHRIST

We believe that Jesus Christ is God incarnate, fully God and fully man, that He was conceived and born of a virgin, lived a sinless life, and offered himself as a penal, substitution sacrifice for sinners.   By the blood of His cross He obtained for us eternal redemption, the forgiveness of sins, and life everlasting.   He was raised bodily on the third day and ascended to the right hand of the Father, there making intercession for the saints, and we believe in His personal, future return to earth.   **Matthew 1:18-25; John 1:1-18; Romans 8:34; 1 Corinthians 15:1-28; 2 Corinthians 5:21; Galatians 3:10-14; Ephesians 1:7; Philippians 2:6-11; Colossians 1:15-23; Hebrews 7:25; 9:13-15; 10:19; 1 Peter 2:21-25; 1 John 2:1-2**

THE HOLY SPIRIT

We believe that the Holy Spirit, the third Person of the Godhead, convicts men of sin, regenerates, baptizes, indwells, seals, and sets apart believers unto a holy life; that He keeps and empowers believers day by day; that He is the Teacher of the Word of God and the Guide for daily living.   Subsequent to conversion the Spirit desires to fill, empower, and anoint believers for ministry and witness.   We also believe that signs and wonders, as well as all the gifts of the Spirit described in the New Testament, are operative today and are designed to testify to the presence of the Kingdom and to empower and edify the church to fulfill its calling and mission.   **Matthew 3:11; John 1:12-13; 3:1-15; Acts 4:29-30; Romans 8:9; 12:3-8; 1 Corinthians 12:12-13; 2 Corinthians 1:21-22; Galatians 3:1-5; Ephesians 1:13-14; 5:18**

MAN

We believe that man was created innocent and pure; and Adam fell through the sin of disobedience.   Therefore, all men are corrupted in body, soul, and spirit; and all men need redemption.   **Genesis 1-3; Psalm 51:5; Isaiah 53:5; Romans 3:9-18; 5:12-21; Ephesians 2:1-3**

SALVATION

We believe that salvation is by grace alone, through faith alone, in Christ alone, a gift of God apart from works.   No ordinance, ritual, work, or any other activity on man's part is required to be saved.   Salvation involves repentance, a change of mind regarding God, and thus turning from one's own way to God's way and is through personal faith in the Lord Jesus Christ.   All who receive Jesus Christ are regenerated by the Holy Spirit and become the children of God.   This saving grace of God, through the power of the Holy Spirit, also sanctifies us by enabling us to do what is pleasing in God's sight so we might be progressively conformed to the image of Christ, and true salvation will be manifested by a changed life.   **John 1:12-13; 6:37-44; 10:25-30; Acts 16:30-31; Romans 3-4; 8:1-17,31-39; 10:8-10; Ephesians 2:8-10; Philippians 2:12-13; Titus 3:3-7; 1 John 1:7,9**

THE FUTURE

We believe in the literal Second Coming of Christ at the end of the age when He will return to the earth personally and visibly to consummate His kingdom.   We also believe in and are praying for a great end-time harvest of souls and the emergence of a victorious church that will experience an unprecedented unity, purity, and power of the Holy Spirit. We believe in the bodily resurrection of the just to the eternal abode in the glory of God's presence, and in the bodily resurrection of the unjust to judgment and everlasting punishment in the lake of fire.   **Psalms 2:7-9; 22:27-28; John 14:12; 17:20-26; Romans 11:25-32; 1 Corinthians 15:20-28,50-58; Ephesians 4:11-16; Philippians 3:20-21; 1 Thessalonians 4:13-5:11; 2 Thessalonians 1:3-12; Revelation 7:9-14; Revelation 11:15**

Let's Begin

If you want a deeper relationship with God, you have to spend quality time with Him.   God will reveal Himself through His Word.   *"Study to shew thyself approved unto God, a workman that needeth not to be ashamed, rightly dividing the word of truth."* **2 Timothy 2:15**

As you begin your study of the Bible, may I suggest you...?

- Be sure to use a good literal word-for-word translation of the Bible, i.e. KJV, NASB, ESV, etc. One with plenty of space that you don't mind marking in.   (Wide-margin Bibles are great!)

- Record what God reveals to you in a journal.   This will result in a deeper, more serious study. It will give you a written record of how God speaks to you and how you responded to Him.

- Use a set of colored pencils or markers to mark "KEY WORDS/PHRASES."

AS NEEDED, USE EXTRA HELPS LIKE:

- **Bible Dictionaries and Encyclopedias**

  - *Bible Dictionaries* discuss & arrange a wide range of Bible subjects alphabetically.

  - A *Bible Encyclopedia* provides more detailed information and articles about a broader range of subjects.

- **Commentaries** are helpful in finding out how other people have understood the Bible. However, if something is not clear, first look up the associated cross-references. If that doesn't clear it up, then see what the commentary has on the passage. This lets you see how others have interpreted the passage.

- **Concordances** are alphabetical lists of all the different words that occur in a book and where they are to be found. It is possible to find where the underlying Greek and Hebrew words have been used even when they have been translated differently in different places in the Bible. These large books are a necessity for serious study.

NOTE: Reference books are helpful, but USE THEM CAREFULLY. Check what they suggest for yourself from the Scriptures.

Acts 17:11

BIBLE STUDIES EASY AS 1, 2, 3...

The right questions, uncover the right answers. When reading God's Word there are **3** questions we must ask ourselves:

(1)"What does it say?"

This is the **observation** of the text and will teach you how to pull out the facts and examine the context.

(2)"What does it mean?"

This is the **interpretation** of the text to discover <u>what</u> it means and what you need to learn.

(3)"How does it apply to me?"

Whether it is a command to obey, a promise to claim, an example to follow, or a sin to confess, the **application** of Bible study deepens our relationship with God.

Observation, interpretation, and application lead to *transformation*. This is the goal at every level of Bible study whether in your daily devotions or the Sunday morning sermon. The ultimate proof that your Bible study method is working is the degree to which it shows in your personal relationship with Him and others.

(1) *Observation* should answer the question:

What does it say?

Ask the 5 W's & H

Who wrote it?

Who did he write it to?

Who are the key characters?

What are the main events?

What is the message?

What are these people like?

When was it written?

When did this event happen?

When did he do or say this?

Where was this written?

Why was this written?

How did it happen?

How did they do it?

How do I do that?

(2) *Interpretation* should answer the questions:

a. What does the passage mean?

b. What does the author mean by what he says?

Remember, always

Interpret Scripture

Considering it's context

(3) *Application* should answer the questions:

a. How does this apply to my life?

b. What truths can I put into practice?

c. What changes should I make?

Survey: *Study each book as a part of the whole. God's plan to redeem men in Christ Jesus runs through the entire Bible. Here are some suggestions to help add more meaning to your study.*

Watch for key words

Consistently marking key words while studying will help you start to identify the themes the author is trying to express.

Keywords always answer the question:

WHO,

WHAT,

WHEN,

WHERE,

WHY

Or

HOW.

Look for the repeated words

Names of key people and their pronouns are key words.

God, Jesus, and Holy Spirit or any words that mean the same, including pronouns, are <u>always</u> key words.

What is the Context?

Context is the environment in which something dwells or the setting where something occurs. Proper *Context* should result in Proper *Interpretation.*

What is the common sense meaning?

How do you solve a puzzle? Look for the obvious, so you can fill in what is missing.

What type of literature is it?

1. History
2. Poetry
3. Prophecy
4. Letter
5. Biographical
6. Doctrine

As easy as...

(1) *Observation* teaches you to see what the passage says.

It is the basis for proper

(2) *Interpretation*

& correct

(3) *Application*.

Accurately observe the text to understand its context. With the right context we determine the true meaning.

Remember to...

Study

Pray first, then read. Trust God for direction & pay attention. Focus your study where He leads.

Observe

Write down words & events that stand out.

Apply

Make it personal. How does this affect your life?

Pray

Pray, listen, and journal your prayers!

LEADING THIS AS A SMALL GROUP BIBLE STUDY?

1. **Pray.** Always start every Bible study by going to God in prayer. Seek an answer from Him. Let Him lead the study. Keep your heart open to hear what He says to you.

2. **Prepare.** Research your topic ahead of time. Get alone with God and into the study of His Word. What does God show you about the subject? Take notes.

3. **Organize.** How much will you cover. Session lengths are guidelines, not requirements. Make an outline and go at your own pace.

4. **Know your audience.** Take into account their Bible knowledge.

5. **Make handouts** for the group. Include the outline you prepared and the relevant scriptures.

6. **Stay on topic.** Don't let the group get distracted or too far off topic, but be sure not to quench the Spirit.

7. **Make it interactive.** Encourage questions. Try to anticipate questions, and address them on your handout with scriptures that back up your answers.

8. **Refill.** Leading a Bible study can take a lot out of you, physically and spiritually. Ask God to pour back into you what was just poured out.

Always remember, allow God to speak through you and your group will always receive what He has for them.

INTRODUCTION

A tale of two cities, two covenants, and two kingdoms

Psalm 24

A Psalm of David.

1 The earth is the Lord's, and the fulness thereof;

The world, and they that dwell therein.

2 For he hath founded it upon the seas,

And established it upon the floods.

3 Who shall ascend into the hill of the Lord?

Or who shall stand in his holy place?

4 He that hath clean hands, and a pure heart;

Who hath not lifted up his soul unto vanity,

Nor sworn deceitfully.

5 He shall receive the blessing from the Lord,

And righteousness from the God of his salvation.

6 *This is the generation of them that seek him,*

That seek thy face, O Jacob. Selah.

7 *Lift up your heads, O ye gates;*

And be ye lift up, ye everlasting doors;

And the King of glory shall come in.

8 *Who is this King of glory?*

The Lord strong and mighty,

The Lord mighty in battle.

9 *Lift up your heads, O ye gates;*

Even lift them up, ye everlasting doors;

And the King of glory shall come in.

10 *Who is this King of glory?*

The Lord of hosts, he is the King of glory. Selah.

Study Kingdom & Covenant. It will change your life, your marriage, and your relationship with God. You will grow in your understanding of who God is and how God is dealing with His people. Are you ready for the journey?

Our Condition

Let's begin at the first two chapters in the Bible. We see that, after creating man, God gave Adam only one commandment. God said, *"Of every tree of the garden thou mayest freely eat: But of the tree of the knowledge of good and evil, thou shalt not eat of it: for in the day that thou eatest thereof thou shalt surely die."* **Genesis 2:16-17**

God expressed His Will to Adam through this commandment. A **sin** is an act which opposes the Will of God. Adam and Eve broke God's commandment and ate the fruit. This was man's first sin. They did something God had told them not to do. They were not obedient to His voice. They acted against His Will. This is where they missed the mark.

Adam questioned God's absolute authority and rejected God's rule over his life by disobeying Him. Adam showed he really did not want to follow God as head of his life. Adam desired to go his own way and follow his own will. He wanted to do, what he wanted to do regardless of what God said.

Since Adam decided he did not want to live under the rule of God, he could no longer rightfully receive the benefits or blessings that came with being under God's rule.   Adam traded the glory of God and the promise of earthly dominion for slavery to sin and the curse of the dominion of death.

Adam was cut off from God's presence and turned out into a hostile land.

Adam was now a *sinner*.

The penalty for sin is *death*.

Adam could do nothing to change the fact that

he had disobeyed God

& he deserved to die.

This sentence of spiritual and physical death was passed on to Adam's children.   Adam and his children were no longer qualified to fulfill the purpose God planned for them when he was created.   To qualify required perfect obedience to God's Will.   Even if Adam lived the rest of his life in perfect obedience, it would not change the fact that he had sinned. It would not change the fact that he had disobeyed God.

For Adam to fulfill the original purpose God had for him and for his children, now someone qualified would have to step in and pay the price.

Adam was in **need** of God's grace.

Adam was in **need** of redemption.

Adam did not **qualify** to redeem himself.

In **Genesis 3:17-18,24** we see Adam's disobedience not only affected his relationship with God, it affected his relationship with everything God gave him authority over.

Sin leads to broken relationships, now Adam's relationship with God was not the same. Now Adam's family and personal relationships were not the same. Now Adam's relationship with the **land** was not the same.

Adam could not restore these broken relationships.

Nothing and no one in all of God's creation was **qualified** to *revive, redeem,* or *restore* man.

God's Response

The "Good News" of the Kingdom

There is some *"good news"* in all of this.   Even before God punished Adam, He promised him a *Seed* that would destroy the works of the serpent (devil) and restore Adam's relationship with God.   This promised *Seed* may suffer, but in the end He will win.   **Genesis 3:15**

God promises that eventually,

By His *grace*,

and for His *purpose*

their *seed* will be revived & redeemed,

and the *Kingdom* will be restored.   **Genesis 3:15**

It is the same *"good news"* that Jesus preached.   It is the *"good news"* that he instructed his disciples to preach.   It is the *"good news"* Paul preached.   It is the *"good news"* of the coming of the **Kingdom of God.**

Jesus taught His disciples to pray *"After this manner therefore pray ye: Our Father which art in heaven, Hallowed be thy name.   Thy **Kingdom** come. Thy will be done in earth, as it is in heaven."* **Matthew 6:9–10**

John the Baptist came *"saying, Repent ye: for the **Kingdom** of heaven is at hand."* **Matthew 3:2**

*"And Jesus went about all Galilee, teaching in their synagogues, and preaching the gospel of the **Kingdom**, and healing all manner of sickness and all manner of disease among the people."* **Matthew 4:23**

*"And Jesus went about all the cities and villages, teaching in their synagogues, and preaching the gospel of the **Kingdom**, and healing every sickness and every disease among the people."* **Matthew 9:35**

*"And this gospel of the **Kingdom** shall be preached in all the world for a witness unto all nations; and then shall the end come."* **Matthew 24:14**

*"Now after that John was put in prison, Jesus came into Galilee, preaching the gospel of the **Kingdom of God**, And saying, The time is fulfilled, and the **Kingdom of God** is at hand: repent ye, and believe the gospel."* **Mark 1:14–15**

*"And when it was day, he departed and went into a desert place: and the people sought him, and came unto him, and stayed him, that he should not depart from them.   And he said unto them, I must preach the **Kingdom of God** to other cities also: for therefore am I sent.   And he preached in the synagogues of Galilee."* **Luke 4:42–44**

*"And it came to pass afterward, that he went throughout every city and village, preaching and shewing the glad tidings of the **Kingdom of God**: and the twelve were with him,"* **Luke 8:1**

*"Then he called his twelve disciples together, and gave them power and authority over all devils, and to cure diseases.   And he sent them to preach the **Kingdom of God**, and to heal the sick."* **Luke 9:1–2**

"The law and the prophets were until John: since that time the **Kingdom of God** *is preached, and every man presseth into it."* **Luke 16:16**

"And when he was demanded of the Pharisees, when the **Kingdom of God** *should come, he answered them and said, The* **Kingdom of God** *cometh not with observation: Neither shall they say, Lo here! or, lo there! for, behold, the* **Kingdom of God** *is within you."* **Luke 17:20–21**

Jesus spent 40 days after His resurrection with his disciples teaching them about the Kingdom.   *"To whom also he shewed himself alive after his passion by many infallible proofs, being seen of them forty days, and speaking of the things pertaining to the* **Kingdom of God:"** **Acts 1:3**

Paul preached the Kingdom of God.

"Confirming the souls of the disciples, and exhorting them to continue in the faith, and that we must through much tribulation enter into the **Kingdom of God.***"* **Acts 14:22**

"And he went into the synagogue, and spake boldly for the space of three months, disputing and persuading the things concerning the **Kingdom of God.***"* **Acts 19:8**

"And when they had appointed him a day, there came many to him into his lodging; to whom he expounded and testified the **Kingdom of God***, persuading them concerning Jesus, both out of the law of Moses, and out of the prophets, from morning till evening."* **Acts 28:23**

"And Paul dwelt two whole years in his own hired house, and received all that came in unto him, Preaching the **Kingdom of God***, and teaching those things which concern the Lord Jesus Christ, with all confidence, no man forbidding him."* **Acts 28:30–31**

God, the Father, *"hath delivered us from the power of darkness, and hath translated us into the **Kingdom** of his dear Son:"* **Colossians 1:13**

The first thing that John saw after God revealed the letters to the churches was God's throne in heaven.   *"And immediately I was in the spirit: and, behold, a throne was set in heaven, and one sat on the throne."* **Revelation 4:2**

When God's Kingdom comes the *"kingdoms of this world"* will become the Kingdoms of our God.

*"And the seventh angel sounded; and there were great voices in heaven, saying, The **kingdoms** of this world are become the **Kingdoms** of our Lord, and of his Christ; and he shall reign for ever and ever."* **Revelation 11:15**

"The gospel of the Kingdom" (**Matthew 4:23**) was preached to Abraham as God's promises. *"And the scripture, foreseeing that God would justify the heathen through faith, preached before the gospel unto Abraham, saying, In thee shall all nations be blessed."* **Galatians 3:8**

Abraham and his descendants have never possessed it. *"These all died in faith, not having received the promises, but having seen them afar off, and were persuaded of them, and embraced them, and confessed that they were strangers and pilgrims on the earth."* **Hebrews 11:13**

However, there will be a resurrection and God's promises will be fulfilled. Abraham and his *seed* will inherit the earth. *"And if ye be Christ's, then are ye Abraham's seed, and heirs according to the promise."* **Galatians 3:29**

In Eden, **Genesis 1:26-30**, we see God establishing His Kingdom and His purpose. Adam, the first man failed to obey God. But Christ, as the *"second Man,"* the *"last Adam"* (**1 Corinthians 15:45-47**) will reign over all the things which the first Adam lost. **Colossians 2:10; Hebrews 2:7-8**

Christ is the "*Seed of the woman*" who will crush the serpent's head. **Genesis 3:15; John 12:31; 1 John 3:8; Galatians 4:4-5**

How this is accomplished is the story the rest of the Bible tells.

DEFINING THE KINGDOM
KINGDOM is about RULER-SHIP

Kingdom

mamlakah מַמְלָכָה

kingdom, sovereignty, dominion, reign

The Bible tells the story of a Kingdom lost and of God's promise to restore and reestablish that Kingdom. It is the story of a people lost and of God's promise to revive and redeem them.

Covenant is the binding commitment which acts as the framework. Covenant establishes the Kingdom relationship. Covenant **defines** the Kingdom.

These are the two central ideas of the Bible, Kingdom and Covenant. They describe how God *rules* and *relates* to His people and His creation.   The Bible is a book about an everlasting *Covenant* and the struggle for an everlasting *Kingdom*.

Kingdom was the message Jesus preached.   It was the message taught and preached by the apostles after Him.   His message was and is the coming of the *"Kingdom of God."*

Jesus declared that He had been sent to preach this message:

*"And when it was day, he departed and went into a desert place: and the people sought him, and came unto him, and stayed him, that he should not depart from them.   And he said unto them, I must preach the **Kingdom of God** to other cities also: for therefore am I <u>sent</u>.   And he preached in the synagogues of Galilee."*

Luke 4:42–44

Jesus taught that:

1. God will establish His **direct** rule or government in the earth through His Son. **Psalms 2**

2. God will establish peace and judge the earth with righteousness. **Psalms 98:9**

3. God will hold every man accountable for the deeds of this life. **Ezekiel 18:4**

4. God will *restore* all things. **Acts 3:21**

5. God will *remove* every curse. **Revelation 22:3**

6. The Son of man will return in the Glory of God. **Matthew 16:27**

7. When the Son of man returns, God's Glory will reside in Jerusalem. **Isaiah 4:5**

8. Every form of human government will be abolished. Every constitution will be voided because the government will *"rest on His shoulders."* **Isaiah 9:6**

9. *" That at the name of Jesus every knee should bow, of things in heaven, and things in earth, and things under the earth; And that every tongue should confess that Jesus Christ is Lord, to the glory of God the Father."* **Philippians 2:10-11**

The foundation of Jesus' message is first found in the book of Genesis. The word *Genesis* is transliterated from the Hebrew word *Bereshith* which means *"in the beginning."* These are the first three words of Scripture. In this book we find the foundation and beginning of all we know about God and His purposes. Genesis gives us our historical point of reference from which all following revelation comes. That is where we will begin our study.

Week 1: What is a Kingdom?

Before we go any further, let's define what a *kingdom* is.

The dictionary defines a kingdom as *"a political or territorial unit ruled by a sovereign."* It is essentially a **nation**, with all of its **citizens**, **land**, and **laws**. It is not only the **reign** or rule of the king, which is expressed by his *will*, but also the **realm** of the king, which is the land and people he governs.

The rule of a king describes his **REIGN,**

or *when* and *how* he rules

REIGN

• the period during which a sovereign occupies the throne.

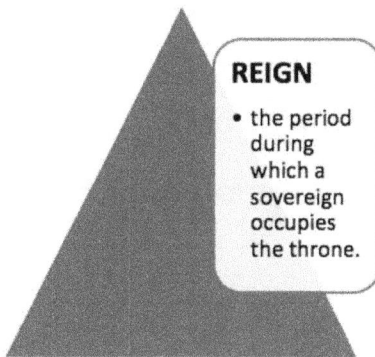

The **Reign** of a king is shown in his sovereign rule and his **power** to exercise his will and authority.

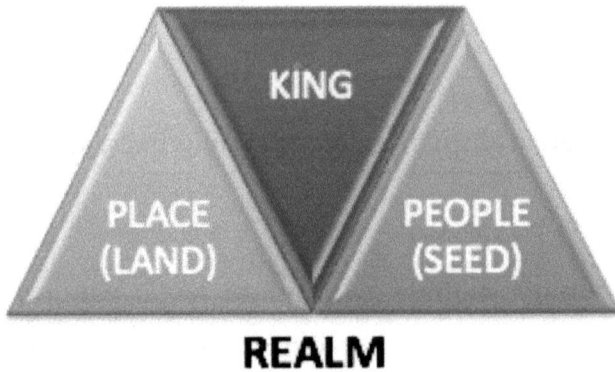

REALM

The **Realm** of a king is the *territory* and people over which the king rules.

A kingdom has four basic parts:

1) A **King**: sovereign or supreme ruler, someone who has absolute, unquestioned authority. He is the only one with the *"right to rule."*

2) A **Place**: land or territory, with its specific location and definite boundary lines.

3) A **People**: subjects or citizens within that territorial jurisdiction.

4) **Order**: The covenant, constitution, laws or a form of government through which the *will* of the ruler is exercised.

In a kingdom the *"right to rule"* was passed down by marriage or birth right. To be the next ruler you had to be connected to the "house" of the king. This referred to the blood line or "seed" of the king. Those who are his direct offspring and *"which shall proceed out of"* the body of the king by birth right. Only members of the royal house could make a claim to their father's throne.

A **King's** *domain* or a **King-dom** establishes:

Who is ruled, or the *people*

Where is ruled, or the *place*

and **how** *order* is maintained

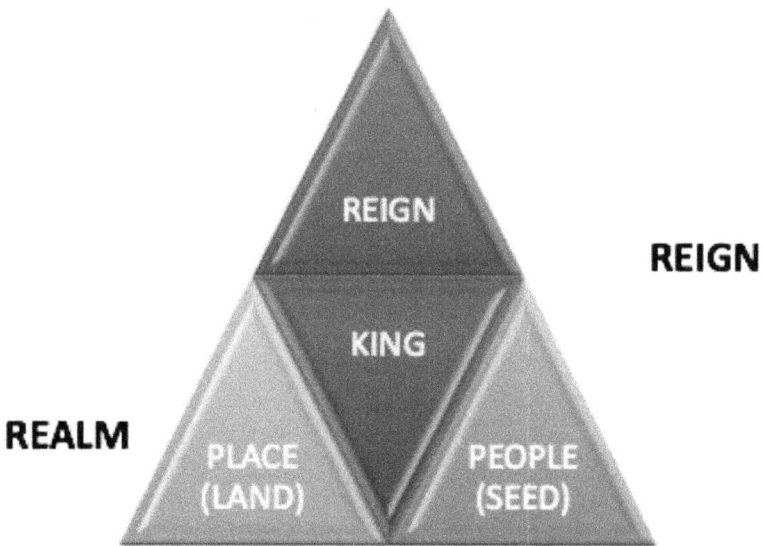

EXAMPLE OF A KINGDOM

So we can say that a kingdom is a *place* and a *people* under the *power* or *authority* of a king.

Because of their position under the *reign* of the king, the *realm*, or *people & place,* receive the *benefits* and the *blessings* that come from being under his reign.

Take note of the following terms, they touch on similar ideas and we will use them interchangeably throughout the upcoming study.

Place and/or *Land*

People and/or *Seed*

Power and/or *Blessing*

The Bible is about a struggle for a Kingdom. The Kingdom of God is mentioned more than 130 times in the New Testament, 102 times just in the Gospels themselves. The *"gospel of the Kingdom"* is the foundation of the **"good news"** Jesus preached.

This **"good news,"** which the Father gave through Jesus Christ, was about His coming **Kingdom** being established on the earth. Jesus Christ brought the **"good news"** about the **Kingdom of God**!

Jesus taught us to pray saying,

"After this manner therefore pray ye:

Our Father which art in heaven, Hallowed be thy name. Thy **Kingdom** *come. Thy will be done in earth, as it is in heaven. Give us this day our daily bread. And forgive us our debts, as we forgive our debtors. And lead us not into temptation, but deliver us from evil: For thine is the* **Kingdom***, and the power, and the glory, for ever. Amen."*

We can summarize His prayer with six "**P's**":

(1) **Privilege:** verse 9   He is *"Our Father"* because:

- *"For ye are all the children of God by faith in Christ Jesus."* **Galatians 3:26**

- *"For ye have not received the spirit of bondage again to fear; but ye have received the Spirit of adoption, whereby we cry, Abba, Father.   The Spirit itself beareth witness with our spirit, that we are the children of God: And if children, then* **heirs; heirs of God, and joint-heirs with Christ***; if so be that we suffer with him, that we may be also glorified together."* **Romans 8:15-16**

- We are adopted by Christ. **Ephesians 1:3-6**

- We are *"no more a servant, but a son."* **Galatians 4:7**

(2) **Purpose:** verse 10 *"Thy* **Kingdom** *come.   Thy will be done in earth, as it is in heaven."*

(3) **Provision:** verse 11 *"Give us this day our daily bread."*

(4) **Peace:** verse 12 *"And forgive us our debts, as we forgive our debtors."*

(5) **Protection:** verse 13 *"And lead us not into temptation, but deliver us from evil:"*

(6) & **Power:** *"For thine is the* **Kingdom***, and the power, and the glory, for ever."*

God has given us His **power** and **authority** through Christ Jesus to accomplish His **purposes** here on earth. **Matthew 28:18-20**

Jesus echoed the prayer of David from **1 Chronicles 29:11-13**.

David prayed this prayer before preparing to build God's temple through his son, Solomon. *"Thine, O Lord, is the greatness, and the power, and the glory, and the victory, and the majesty: for all that is in the heaven and in the earth is thine; thine is the **Kingdom**, O Lord, and thou art exalted as head above all."* **1 Chronicles 29:11-13**

1. **Read Matthew 6:7-15 :** What do we mean when we pray, "Thy Kingdom Come?"

2. **Read Matthew 4:17-25 :** What do you think was the "good news" of the Kingdom Jesus preached?

3. **Read Luke 19:1-10 :** For what purpose did the Son of Man come?

Week 2: Kingdom Purpose & Provision

Read Genesis 1 and 2

1. Do these chapters describe a *"kingdom"* as defined in Week 1?

2. If so, who would inherit this *"kingdom"*?

In the first two chapters of Genesis, we see that God creates and enters into a relationship with Adam and Eve.   He promised them that their *seed* would inherit the *earth*.

In **Genesis 1:26-30**, we see that God created man for His Glory and to *"fill the earth"* and to *"have dominion"* over it. **Genesis 1:27,28**

Let's dig deeper for a moment and look at **Genesis 1:26-28**.

*"And God said, Let us make man in our **image**, after our likeness: and let them have **dominion** over the fish of the sea, and over the fowl of the air, and over the cattle, and **over all the earth**, and over every creeping thing that creepeth upon the earth.*

*So God created man in his own **image**, in the **image** of God created he him; male and female created he them.*

*And God blessed them, and God said unto them, Be fruitful, and multiply, and replenish the earth, and subdue it: and have **dominion** over the fish of the sea, and over the fowl of the air, and over every living thing that moveth upon the earth."*

The Bible tells us that God is Creator and King over all the earth and creation. **Psalms 24**

God created Adam to represent His rule over all the earth. **Genesis 1:26**

God gave Adam the *authority* to properly represent Him and His Glory and His reign over His creation.

We can see, from verse 27, that God created man in His own *image*. Also we see here from the 28th verse that God created man to *"fill the earth"*, to *"subdue"* it, and to *"have dominion"* over the earth.

Adam was to spread his *seed* throughout the *land,* to the glory of God, and *"have dominion"* over the *land.* God's purpose was to *fill the earth* and all of creation with His *Glory* through man's representation.

In the first two chapters of Genesis, we see three things emphasized:

A **Land** that extends to the corners of the earth,

A **Seed** that includes all the families of the earth,

& the **Blessing** of God's presence.

This is the created Kingdom of God, which is composed of the same three elements, a *Place* of God, a *People* of God, governed by the *Power* of God.

These three,

the *Land,*

the *Seed,*

& the *Blessing,*

all added up to the *Kingdom* of God on earth.

Week 3: Kingdom Promise

Lets review for a moment.

God gave Adam only one commandment to keep saying, "*Of every tree of the garden thou mayest freely eat: But of the tree of the knowledge of good and evil, thou shalt not eat of it: for in the day that thou eatest thereof thou shalt surely die.*" **Genesis 2:16-17**

1) This commandment expressed God's Will for Adam.

2) Adam and Eve broke His commandment and ate of the fruit.

3) By doing this Adam rejected God's rule over his life.

4) This meant Adam could no longer rightfully receive the benefits or the blessings associated with being under God's rule.

5) Adam exchanged the glory of God and earthly dominion for slavery to sin and the dominion of death.

6) The spread of man would no longer mean the spread of God's Kingdom.

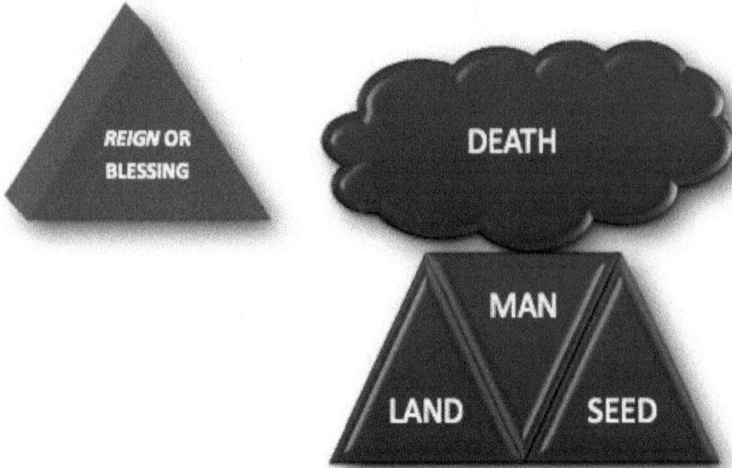

Worse yet, Adam could not restore his broken relationships. He was not **qualified**.   No one was **qualified** to redeem man.

So, God obligated Himself to restore the relationship and fulfill the promise regardless of man's response and not dependent upon him to fulfill any conditions.

 God promises that eventually,

By His *grace,*

and for His *purpose*

He will revive and redeem their **seed,**

and **He** will restore the Kingdom.   **Genesis 3:15**

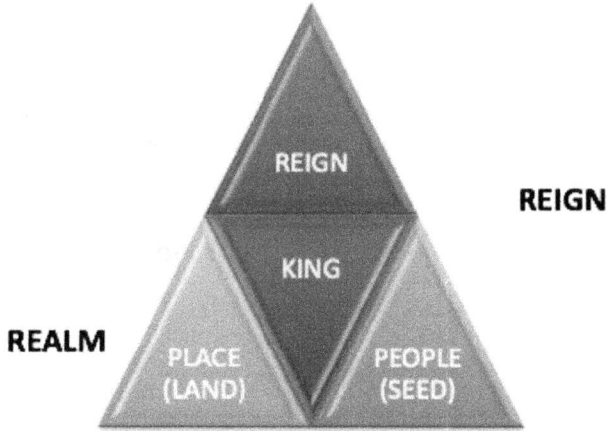

God promises that the **Reign** and **Realm** will be

Revived, Redeemed, & Restored.

Although this would not come without great struggle. Everything now would be a struggle.

Now Adam would struggle to produce the fruit of the *land*.

Now Eve would struggle to give birth to their *seed*.

Now they no longer existed under God's *blessing*.

But everything is not lost, God promises a *Seed*. **Genesis 3:15**

This **Seed** would destroy the works of the devil. He would revive, redeem and restore man's relationship with God. The promised **Seed** may suffer, but in the end He will triumph.

The promised **Seed** was from God and He would be preserved by God. Adam sins, but God promises restoration and redemption.

In **Genesis 3:15**, Adam and Eve heard God tell the serpent about the coming **Seed** saying, *"it shall bruise thy head, and thou shalt bruise his heel."* There must have been a sense of expectation when Eve soon gave birth to Cain and Abel. But the wickedness of Cain led him to kill Abel. Yet and still, God keeps the promise and continues the **Seed** through Seth. **Genesis 4:25-26**

As time passes, God sees *"the wickedness of man was great on the earth and that every imagination of man's heart was evil,"* so God chooses to destroy and purify the earth with a flood. Yet and still, God preserves the **Seed**, by preserving Noah. **Genesis 6:5-22 & 9**

Read Genesis 6:5-22 & 9

1. Why did God destroy the earth?

2. What did God make with Noah?

3. Why?

On the other side of the flood, God continues to preserve of the *Seed* through Noah's son Shem. God fills the earth with his children and forms the first nations. The citizens of the nations were meant to be the heirs of the Kingdom. **Genesis 10**

Read Genesis 11:1-9

4. How does the story of the Tower of Babel relate to the Kingdom of God?

Notice how, at the Tower of Babel, instead of filling the earth with God's glory and glorifying His Name, the wickedness of man leads him to seek to make a name for himself and establish a kingdom of his own.

This is a kingdom in conflict with God's Kingdom.   It is the first of the *"kingdoms of this world"*.   It is a city and kingdom called *Babylon*.   **Genesis 11:1-9**

Read Genesis 12:1-3

5. What was Abraham commanded to do?

To preserve the *Seed* and the promise, God calls Abraham out of *"Ur of the Chaldees"* to set apart a people to Himself. *"Ur of the Chaldees"* was part of Ancient Babylonia, so Abraham was called out of Babylon.

God preserved the *Seed* through Abraham and Sarah by allowing them to give birth in their old age. The promised *Seed* would come through Isaac, not Ishmael; Jacob, and not Esau.

God preserved the *Seed*

through Isaac in **Genesis 26,**

through Jacob in **Genesis 28,**

& through Judah in **Genesis 49.**

OF WOMAN | OF SETH | OF SHEM | OF ABRAHAM | OF ISAAC | OF JACOB | OF JUDAH | OF DAVID

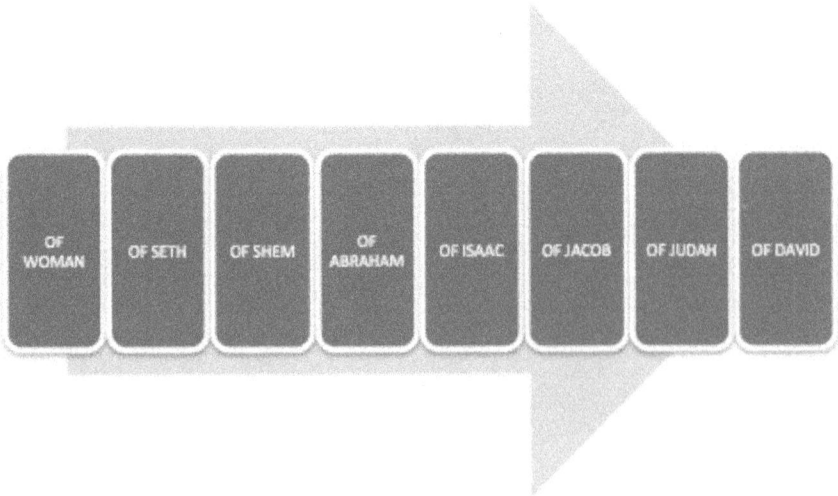

TRAIL OF THE *"SEED"*

Finally, in Genesis we see that this Seed will be Israel's coming ruler and would be from the tribe of Judah: *"The sceptre shall not depart from Judah, nor a lawgiver from between his feet, until Shiloh come; and unto him shall the gathering of the people be."* **Genesis 49:10**

Prophecy after prophecy, God provides us a picture so that when the promised *Seed* arrives on the scene His identity will be unmistakable. Here are just a few of those prophecies:

Genesis 3:15; 12:3; 49:10 ....**The Promise**

Exodus 12:40-50 ....**The Passover Lamb**

Numbers 24:17..**The Scepter**

Deuteronomy 18:17-19...............................**The Coming Prophet**

Job 19:25-27..**The Resurrection**

Psalms:
2:1-12 ....**The World Order to be Destroyed**
8:1-9 ....**Brought low to suffer death**
16:7-11..**Will not see decay**
22:1-31 ....**The Crucifixion Foretold**
45:1-9 ....**The King and His Bride**
110:1-7 ....**The Coming Priest**

Proverbs 30:4 ....**The Son**

Isaiah:

7:14 ....To be Born of a Virgin

9:6-7 ....The Man who is God

11:1-5 ....The Righteous Judge

42:1-9...The Judge of the Nations

49:5-7 ....The Light of the Gentiles

52:13-15 ....The Suffering Servant

53:1-12 ....Lamb of God, resurrected

Jeremiah 31:31-34 ....The New Covenant

Daniel:

7:13-14..His Kingdom is Forever

9:26..He is to be "cut off" (initially)

Amos   8:9-10.. Sun to go down at Noon

Micah 5:2 ....The Christ to be born in Bethlehem

Zechariah:

9:9 ....King to enter Jerusalem riding a donkey (1st Coming)

11:10-13 ....He is to be sold for 30 pieces of silver

12:9-10 ....Repentance of the Jews (2nd Coming)

14:1-9 ....The Second Coming

Malachi 3:1-5............................. A messenger prepares the way

A TALE OF TWO CITIES
Where do you live?

Babylon or Jerusalem

The Bible speaks of two cities, Babel and Jerusalem. One devoted to man, the other ruled by God. One focused on self, the other focused on God. These two cities represent two ways of life.

Babel is the first city of any size mentioned in the Bible. **Genesis 11:1-9**

It is on the plain of Shinar and is also known as **"Babylon."** Babel is a city where the people are focused on themselves and their desires. Babel is the city of man.

There is another city where things are different. **Jerusalem** is known as *"Zion"* or the *"City of David."* It is the resting place of the Ark of the Covenant which represents God's presence with his people. It is the city where the Temple of Solomon was built and blessed with God's presence. It is the place from which God rules His world. Jerusalem is God's City.

Jerusalem and Babylon are the most mentioned cities in the Bible. Babylon is the result of man's lack of faith, but Jerusalem is the result of God's call of a man of faith to make His plan of salvation available to the world.

The story of Tower of Babel teaches us that, despite all man's efforts, God's purpose will ultimately be accomplished.

To be aligned with God's purpose will mean

Life,

Salvation

& the **Blessing**.

To oppose His purpose will mean

Death,

Judgment

& the **Curse**.

Week 4: Babylon

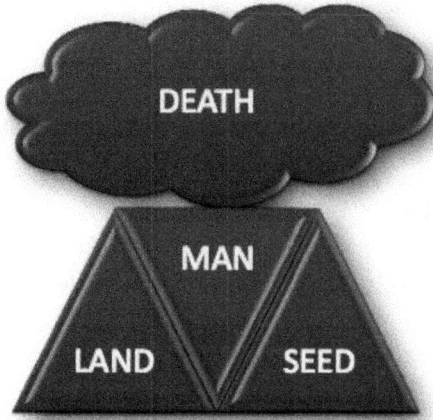

Babylon (Hebrew *Babel)* represents independence, pride and rebellion. It is the place where man seeks to **exalt his own name** and **live according to his own will**.

The very first mention of **Babel** in the Bible is in **Genesis 10:8-10**. It would later be called Babylon. **Genesis 10:10; 11:1-9**

Babylon was founded by Nimrod, whose name means *"Let us revolt or rebel."* His nature and character are seen both in his name and in the city he founded. In **Genesis 11:4**, we see Nimrod's kingdom, Babylon, becoming a place and a *name* for those who oppose God and His kingdom.

In **Genesis 11**, we see the people of **"the land of Shinar"** have one language. This land is lower Mesopotamia or Babylon, also called Chaldea. The people built a *"fortified tower"* designed to reach the heavens. They desired to make it to heaven on their own terms and by their own merits.

Read Genesis 11: 1-4

1. What does **Genesis 11:1** say about earth before the Tower of Babel?

2. Do you see this changing in our world today? Why or why not?

According to Scripture, the people said:

> "Go to, **let us** make brick, and burn them thoroughly.   And they had brick for stone, and slime had they for mortar.   And they said, Go to, **let us** build **us** a city and a tower, whose top may reach unto heaven; and **let us** make **us** a **name**, lest **we** be scattered abroad upon the face of the whole earth." **Genesis 11:3,4**

3. What was the purpose of the *"tower"* ?

4. Would the Lord be pleased with it?

5. Why or why not?

Notice they say *"let us."* **Genesis 3** was about individual sin, but here we see all the people unified under the same sin and for the same evil purpose. They don't want to be scattered as God commanded in **Genesis 10**, so they decide to organize themselves apart from God to resist His will. They seek their own authority, not God's authority. They seek their own will, not God's Will. They say in their heart, "Not thy Will, but *my* will be done."

Read Genesis 11:5-9

6. What did God do in **Genesis 11:5**?

7. What did God observe?

8. What did He do next?

9. Why? **Genesis 11:6**

God says, *"Go to, LET US go down, and there confound their language, that they may not understand one another's speech."* **Genesis 11:7**

Notice, the *"LET US"* of God overcomes the *"let us"* of man. God judged their desires and confused their language. The city and the tower were left unfinished. **Genesis 11:5-8**

According to **Genesis 11:9** it was *"called Babel; because the Lord did there confound the language of all the earth: and from thence did the Lord scatter them abroad upon the face of all the earth."* Babylon still symbolizes opposition to God's Will.

After **Genesis 11**, there are no direct references to Babylon until the prophecies of Isaiah, Jeremiah, Ezekiel, and Daniel.

Week 5: Jerusalem

Jerusalem represents people living under God's authority. It is a place of unity under the authority of God. Jerusalem is the place where God placed His **Name** and His dwelling. **Deuteronomy 16:2; 1 Chronicles 21:28-29; 22:1-5**

Abram was called to leave *Ur of the Chaldees* and look for another city. A city with foundations, *"whose builder and maker is God."* **Hebrews 11:8-10**

His journey goes from Genesis to Revelation. **Genesis 1-11** tells the story from "the fall" to "the call." With the call of Abraham a new chapter begins. The rest of the Bible is about God's plan to revive, redeem and restore His creation. To create a New Heaven and a New Earth filled with His Glory and His righteousness.

Read Genesis 14:18-20

1. Who did Abraham pay tithes to?

2. What was he the King of?

Read Genesis 22

3. What was Abraham willing to sacrifice?

4. Where did God tell Abraham to offer up his son?

After David became king of all Israel he captured Jerusalem and made it his capital city (**2 Samuel 5:6-10**), the *"City of David"*. It was near the border, between Judah and Benjamin. David's choice of Jerusalem as his capital unified the kingdom. Jerusalem, *"the City of the Great King"*, now represented the unity of God's people.

Read 1 Chronicles 21 - 22:1-5

Here pride led David to conduct a census of Israel to determine the strength of his army. **1 Chronicles 21:1-2**

David repented and God did not destroy Jerusalem. It was at this time God chose to reveal the place where He would be worshipped. **1 Chronicles 21:18-22:5**

Read 2 Chronicles 3:1

5. Where did Solomon build the Temple?

6. At what city?

7. On what mountain?

NOTE: This is the same place where Abraham had been prepared to offer Isaac in **Genesis 22**.

Read Isaiah 6:1-4

Isaiah had a vision of God in that same Temple.

8.   What was *"the whole earth is full of ..."*?

9. Does this sound similar to God's original purpose to *fill the earth* and all of creation with His *Glory*?

Week 6: From Babel to Pentecost

David died and was buried in *Jerusalem*.   **1 Kings 2:10**

On the Day of Pentecost, Peter said, *"His tomb is with us to this day."* **Acts 2:29**

Jesus died and was buried in *Jerusalem*, but He also rose from the dead and ascended to heaven in *Jerusalem*, just as David had prophesied.   **Psalm 16:9-10** and **Acts 2:24-32**

Jesus commanded the disciples to wait in *Jerusalem* to *"receive power, after that the Holy Ghost is come upon you."* **Acts 1:4-5,8** The message of the Kingdom would go forth from Jerusalem to the ends of the earth.   **Acts 1:6-8**

Is there a connection between Babel and Pentecost? If the answer is yes, then understanding this connection can help us better understand God's purpose.

Read Acts 2

1. Who was dwelling at Jerusalem? How many nations?

2. Do you see any relationship between the *"one language, and of one speech"* of **Genesis 11** and speaking in tongues in **Acts 2**? Think about it.

In **Acts 2**, under the influence of the Holy Spirit, Peter preached in a language that everyone understood. The judgment of Babel was reversed. There was a table of nations listed just like in **Genesis 10**. The filling of the Holy Ghost removed the curse of Babel with the *"gift of tongues"* and *"every man heard them speak in his own language..."* *"the wonderful works of God."* **Acts 2:6-11**

In Genesis, God punished and divided the people, *confounding* their speech and spreading them throughout the world. However, in **Acts 2**, men were cofounded that they could understand one another. God used the *"gift of tongues"* as a means to gather the people of God and use them to spread the message of His Kingdom throughout the world.

Acts 2 brings together 3 Old Testament ideas:

1) The reverse of the curse of Babel. **Genesis 11**

2) The empowering by God of the believer through His Spirit to obey the Law. **Jeremiah 31:31-34**

3) The beginning of the Abraham's blessing where he was promised that, *"in thee shall all families of the earth be blessed."* **Genesis 12:3**

3. What significance does unity have on the body of Christ? **Genesis 11:6; Acts 2:44-45; Acts 4:32-33**

4. How do you personally do in the area of unity?

5. Are you of *"singleness of heart"* with the believers in your church? Why or why not?

This world is once again becoming a "one-world" culture through technology, the media, the internet and the "world wide web". God originally confounded man's speech to restrain man's wickedness. God saw the problems that occur when men unite for evil purposes. However, when God's purposes for this old world are done, there will be a new heaven and a new earth.

Revelation 21-22 describes this New Jerusalem. This holy city, *"coming down from God out of heaven"*, is the direct opposite of man's desire at Babel to *"build us a city and a tower, whose top may reach unto heaven."* The New Jerusalem will fulfill all that the earthly Jerusalem was meant to.

COVENANT DEFINED
COVENANT is about RELATIONSHIP

"Forasmuch as ye know that ye were not redeemed with corruptible things, as silver and gold, from your vain conversation received by tradition from your fathers;

But with the precious blood of Christ, as of a lamb without blemish and without spot:

Who verily was foreordained before the foundation of the world, but was manifest in these last times for you," **1 Peter 1:18-20**

Covenant

berith ברית

A covenant

What is a Covenant?

A covenant is a solemn binding agreement between two parties. Everything God does with mankind is based on the covenant.

Covenants are referred to as **blood covenants** for a reason. Blood sealed the agreement. Covenant is about **blood**. It is about a blood covering, a blood connection and a blood commitment.

> *"And almost all things are by the law purged with blood; and without shedding of blood is no remission."* **Hebrews 9:22**

Blood covenants represent a bond between two parties that cannot be broken. The *blood* refers to the blood of the animal sacrificed or *"cut."*

This blood represented the animal giving up its life. This sacrificed *substitute* satisfied, or made *atonement* for, the human sins it represented. *"For the life of the flesh is in the blood, and I have given it to you upon the altar to make atonement for your souls; for it is the blood that makes atonement for the soul."* **Leviticus 17:11**

Where did covenant begin?

God made a covenant with Noah.

God made a covenant with Abram.

God reaffirmed that covenant with Isaac, then Jacob.

From the very beginning we see God's *progressive revelation* of His purpose to revive, redeem and restore His people and His Kingdom. God does not show us everything all at once. God begins with the basics, then builds on this foundation to reveal a larger truth. He establishes the foundation and fundamentals before revealing the whole matter.

The New Testament takes the Old Testament idea of sacrifice and applies it to the blood of Christ. Any references to the *"blood of Christ"* always refer to His death and sacrifice on the cross.

Paul, (**Romans 3:25**)

Peter, (**1 Peter 1:19**)

John, (**Revelation 1:5**)

& the author of Hebrews. (**Hebrews 9:14**)

Each preached about the power of His blood. Though all have sinned, *"We have redemption through His blood, the forgiveness of sins."* **Ephesians 1:7**

When we enter into this blood covenant we receive the **protection**, the **provision** and the **peace** bought by the blood of Christ. Understanding what the covenants mean, how they are made, the signs and the symbols of the covenants will be the key to understanding the Bible as a whole. This understanding opens up Genesis and the entire Bible. It reveals God's plan for the world.

Week 7: *Blood* Covered

God is a God of covenant. **Psalms 111:9; Hebrews 6:12-17**

There are two kinds of covenants between God and man in Scripture,

The conditional and unconditional.

Read Exodus 19:5; Deuteronomy 28:58,59: This is conditional. There are conditions to fulfill and commands to obey.   God says only *"If..."* we obey the conditions *"then..."* he will provide the promises.   It is solely dependent upon man's obedience.

Read Exodus 6:3-8; Genesis 9:11: These are unconditional. God says simply, *"I will"* and obligates Himself to fulfill the promises of the covenant no matter what our response is and not dependent upon our participation.

To *"cut a covenant"* involved a process.   Some important parts of this process can be seen in the covenant made between Laban and Jacob in **Genesis 31:25-54.**

Read Genesis 31:43-55 *Jacob with Laban*

1. What steps did Jacob and Laban take to *"cut"* a covenant? Try to list them.

Did you see...

     i. An agreement of the **terms. Genesis 31:49-52**

    ii. The swearing of an **oath. Genesis 53**

   iii. The offering of a **sacrifice. Genesis 31:54** *Blood sealed the agreement.*

   iv. The **witness** or **sign. Genesis 31:46-48,51-52**

    v. The **feast. Genesis 31:54**

Read Genesis 15

2.   What was cut?

3.   What was shed?

4.   After the cutting was done, what happened?

Week 8: *Blood* Connected

We were created to be in relationship with God.   When Adam and Eve sinned, they broke fellowship and relationship with God.   But, God already had a plan of salvation that would revive, redeem and restore His children to himself. God's plan, His *"eternal purpose,"* was set *from the foundation of the world.*

God had already worked out His purpose and guaranteed our relationship.   It is this **purpose** and this **promise** that are progressively revealed through all God's covenants.

The people of the Bible understood covenants.   They made promises and expected benefits.   If the promises were broken, they expected penalties based on the terms of the covenant. Covenant established and defined the relationship between the covenant parties.

TO BE IN COVENANT IS TO BE IN RELATIONSHIP.

1. COVENANTS RESOLVE CONFLICTS:

Abraham made a covenant with the Philistine king Abimelech to resolve their conflict over a well. **Genesis 21:22-34**

2. COVENANTS ESTABLISH FRIENDSHIPS:

David and Jonathan made a covenant that established their everlasting friendship and that confirmed David's right to the throne of Israel. **1 Samuel 18:3** and **23:18**

3. COVENANTS PROVIDE PROTECTION & PROVISION:

Jacob and Laban, made a covenant promise never to harm each other and Jacob promised to provide for Laban's daughters. **Genesis 31:43-53**

One of the keys to understanding God's plan for our *relationship* in covenant lies in the institution of marriage.

"And the Lord God caused a deep sleep to fall upon Adam, and he slept: and he took one of his ribs, and closed up the flesh instead thereof;

And the rib, which the Lord God had taken from man, made he a woman, and brought her unto the man.

And Adam said, This is now bone of my bones, and flesh of my flesh: she shall be called Woman, because she was taken out of Man.

*Therefore shall a man leave his father and his mother, and shall cleave unto his wife: and **they shall be one flesh.**"*

Genesis 2:21-24

THEY SHALL BE ONE FLESH.

This **intimacy**, this **oneness** and **union** is the essence of what a covenant is all about. Covenant partners viewed each other as friends, *forever*. The covenant relationship is based on friendship and established by the covenant.

This friendship, once established, entitled each partner access to what the other possesses.   Each has an effective *"power of attorney"* and can act in the **name** of the other party.

We can see this in **1 Samuel 18:1-4**, which uses **an *exchange of robes*** to symbolize this union.   Here, the robe or coat represents the identity and authority of the one entering this covenant.   By exchanging robes, Jonathan and David symbolically showed their love, connection, commitment and unity.

Read 1 Samuel 17:55-18:9

1. Why did Jonathan make a covenant with David?

2. What things did Jonathan give David when he made a covenant with him?

3. Why?

Read Galatians 3:26-27

4. Who is being described?

5. What happens to all who have been baptized into Christ?

Read Ephesians 4:20-24

6. What do we do with the *"old self"*?

7. What do we do with the *"new self"*?

8. Does the *"put off"* and *"put on"* of Galatians and Ephesians remind you of Jonathan and David's exchange of robes? If so, how?

Marriage is God's perfect example of covenant and relationship. God uses it to demonstrate the essence of what that relationship should mean.

God views His people as a husband views a wife. **Hosea 2:16,19; Isaiah 62:1-5; Matthew 9:15 & 22:1-14;** and **Revelation 19:7**

He also views idolatry as adultery. **Jeremiah 3:8**

In marriage:

1. *Two lives become one,*

2. *There is a partner to defend,*

3. *There is a sign to serve as a witness, (ring)*

4. *There is a change of name,*

5. *There is an exchange of vows,*

6. *There is a meal shared,*

7. *There is a friend that will stick closer than a brother.*

Read Genesis 17:5,15; 32:18

9. What did God change their names to?

10. Why?

Abram became Abraham.   Sarai became Sarah.   Just as in marriage the wife takes on the name of the husband, they took a part of God's name (in Hebrew: *YHWH*) and added to their own.   They were intimately connected.

Week 9: *Blood* Committed

A *covenant* is primarily an *agreement* or commitment between two people or two groups that involves promises to one another.

The idea of *a covenant* between God and His people is one of the most important truths of the Bible. Covenant defines the relationship between the King and citizens within the Kingdom. It also expresses and identifies the King's Will. It is the law of the land.

Covenant **defines** the Kingdom.

Covenant **ushers** in the Kingdom.

Covenant **sustains** the Kingdom.

By making a covenant with Abraham, God promised to provide him a *land* and *bless* his *seed*. Abraham, however, must be faithful and allow God to use him as a vessel through which His blessings would flow to the rest of the world. **Genesis 12:1-3**

Let us look briefly at an example of a covenant to better understand them and their use in the Bible.

Genesis 6:18 is the first appearance in the Bible of the word *"BERYTH,"* which is the Hebrew word translated *"covenant"*. God offers Noah and his family a *"covenant"*, which looks like what we might call a *"contract"*.

Read Genesis 6:5-22 & 9

1. Is this covenant between Noah and God different from our contracts?

2. What do you think were the terms of the covenant between Noah and God?

3. If Noah had not committed himself to obey God, would they still have had a covenant relationship?

4. Was there a sign or *token* of this covenant? If so, what was it and what was its purpose?

Covenant is a binding commitment. It acts as the framework for the relationship. Much like the Constitution establishes the framework for a nation. Its promise guarantees the same things all citizens expect from any government: provision, peace, and protection. God's Covenant defines His relationship with us.

For those who remain faithful and committed to the King, ...

It promises to **Protect.**

It promises to **Provide.**

It promises of **Peace.**

It promises His **Presence.**

And in time of trouble,

It assures **Salvation.**

That is why the believer can say He is...

Jehovah-Nissi - *"The-LORD-Is-My-Banner."* **Exodus 17:15-16**

Jehovah-Jireh - *"The-LORD-Will-Provide,"* from the provision of the ram in place of Isaac for Abraham's sacrifice. **Genesis 22:8,14**

Jehovah-Shalom - *"The-LORD-Is-Peace"* the name Gideon gave the altar which he built in Ophrah. **Judges 6:23-24**

Jehovah-Shamah - *"The-LORD-Is-There"* referring to the city which the prophet Ezekiel saw in his vision. **Ezekiel 48:35**

Jehovah-Tsebaoth - *"The-LORD-of-hosts"* was used in the days of David and the prophets to witness to God the Savior who is surrounded by His hosts of heavenly armies. He is the "Commander-in-Chief" of the armies of heaven. **Amos 4:13; Isaiah 6:3; 31:4-5; 44:6**

The king commits to **protect** the people and their borders from outside invaders.   He commits to ensure **peace** and stability exists within the land.   He also commits to **provide** for and make sure to meet His subjects every need.   However, to receive the benefits they must commit and submit to the will of the king.

Covenant involves a commitment to protect the other person. The belt holds the weapons. The exchange of belts shows that the covenant parties are allies and will come to each others aid in time of trouble.

Re-read 1 Samuel 18:1-4

5. What else did Jonathan give David besides his robe?

6. Why do you think he did this?

Read Ephesians 6:10-17

7. Whose armor should we wear?

8. Why?

9. List the pieces of the armor from **Ephesians 6:10-17**, also list the verse and what each represents:

10. Are you wearing each of these daily?

THE PROMISES OF GOD

"For, behold, I create new heavens and a new earth: And the former shall not be remembered, nor come into mind. But be ye glad and rejoice for ever in that which I create: For, behold, I create Jerusalem a rejoicing, and her people a joy." **Isaiah 65:17-18**

"For as the new heavens and the new earth, which I will make, Shall remain before me, saith the Lord, So shall your seed and your name remain." **Isaiah 66:22**

Genesis *is* the **book of origins**, and forms the root of every following revelation of God. Every theme of the Bible flows like a river from this source.

The first eleven Chapters of Genesis can be seen by four major events:

The Creation *chapters 1-2,*

The Fall *chapters 3-5,*

The Flood *chapters 6-9,*

& Tower of Babel *chapter 11.*

The remaining chapters of Genesis, 12-50, deal with four main characters and the unfolding of a promise:

to Abraham **12:1 - 25:18,**

to Isaac **25:19 - 26:35,**

to Jacob **27 - 36,**

and to Joseph **37 - 50.**

The promise which is unfolded is God's covenant with Abraham. It is the framework of what is revealed in the Bible. It is the unifying principle. The Old testament saints looked forward to this promise. The promise made to us is the same promise made to them. There is one gospel, one way to salvation, and one central message in the Bible. It is found in the covenant God made with Abraham. It is founded on the blood of Christ. Just as if the sacrifice had been made before the foundation of the world.

Week 10: Abraham's Covenant

" *By faith Abraham, when he was called to go out* [from Ur of the Chaldees] *into a place which he should after receive for an inheritance, obeyed; and he went out, not knowing whither he went. By faith he sojourned in the land of promise, as in a strange country, dwelling in tabernacles with Isaac and Jacob, the heirs with him of the same promise: For he looked for a city which hath foundations, whose builder and maker is God.*" **Hebrews 11:8-10**

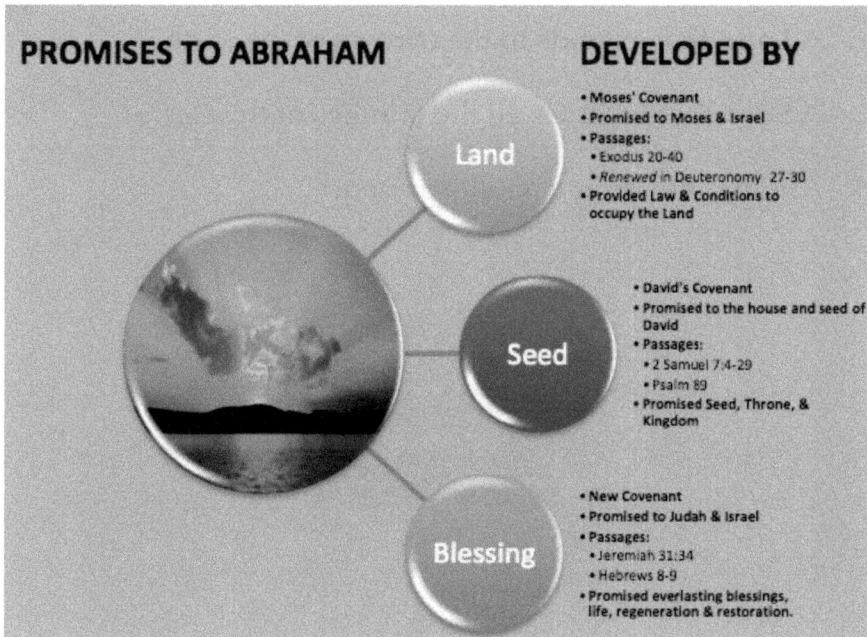

God begins narrowing things down. He moves from all people to one specific person. The focus is, for now, on one specific land, and one specific seed that will receive God's unique and special blessing. God's covenant with Abraham is the first mention of that covenant. Everything that follows is simply the unfolding, the working out and the fulfilling of the covenant God made with Abraham. Remember, the purpose of promised *land* and promised *seed* are to revive, redeem and restore the *blessing* to all the families and all the nations of all the earth. **Genesis 10**

God's promises to Abraham address three things:

1. A **Land** that extends to the corners of the earth,

2. A **Seed** that includes all the families of the earth,

3. And the **Blessing** of God's presence.

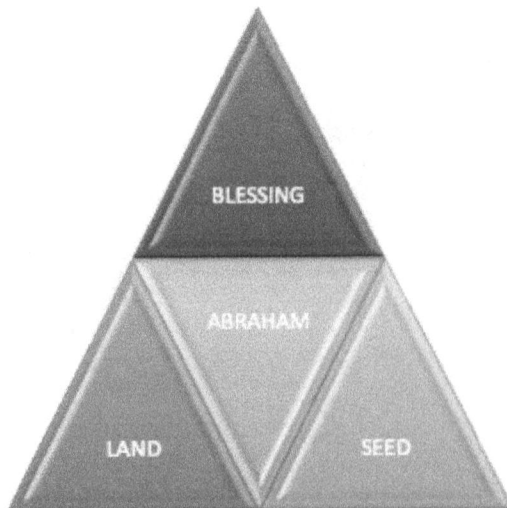

"Now the Lord had said unto Abram,

Get thee out of thy country, and from thy kindred, and from thy father's house,

*unto a **land** that I will shew thee:*

*And I will make of thee a great **nation**,*

*and I will **bless** thee,*

and make thy name great;

and thou shalt be a blessing:

And I will bless them that bless thee, and curse him that curseth thee:

*and in **thee shall all families of the earth be blessed**."*

Genesis 12:1-3

Do you see the familiar themes of *land, seed,* and *blessing*?

1. When God spoke, Abram moved. Why do you think God wanted Abram to leave his familiar surroundings?

The Land

"Now the Lord had said unto Abram, Get thee out of thy country, and from thy kindred, and from thy father's house, unto a **land** that I will shew thee:" **Genesis 12:1**

"And the Lord said unto Abram, after that Lot was separated from him, Lift up now thine eyes, and look from the place where thou art northward, and southward, and eastward, and westward: For all the **land** which thou seest, **to thee will I give it,** and to thy seed for ever." **Genesis 13:14-15**

"In the same day the Lord made a covenant with Abram, saying, Unto thy seed have I given this land, from the river of Egypt unto the great river, the river Euphrates:" **Genesis 15:18**

"And I will give unto thee, and to thy seed after thee, the land wherein thou art a stranger, all the **land** of Canaan, for an everlasting possession; and I will be their God." **Genesis 17:8**

"For the **promise**, that he should be the **heir of the world**, was not to Abraham, or to his seed, through the law, but through the righteousness of faith." **Romans 4:13**

Read Genesis 15 & 17:1-24

2. What did God promise? To whom?

3. Why was Abraham accounted righteous?

4. What did Abraham believe? **See Galatians 3:6-8**

> *"Even as Abraham believed God, and it was accounted to him for righteousness.   Know ye therefore that they which are of faith, the same are the children of Abraham.   And the scripture, foreseeing that God would justify the heathen through faith, preached before the* **gospel** *unto Abraham, saying,* **In thee shall all nations be blessed.**" **Galatians 3:6-8**

The Seed

"*And I will make of thee a great nation, and I will bless thee, and make thy name great; and thou shalt be a blessing: And I will bless them that bless thee, and curse him that curseth thee: and in thee shall all families of the earth be blessed.*" **Genesis 12:2-3**

"*For all the land which thou seest, to thee will I give it, **and to thy seed for ever**. And I will make thy **seed** as the dust of the earth: so that if a man can number the dust of the earth, then shall thy **seed** also be numbered.*" **Genesis 13:15-16**

"*And he brought him forth abroad, and said, Look now toward heaven, and tell the stars, if thou be able to number them: and he said unto him, So shall thy seed be. And he believed in the Lord; and he counted it to him for righteousness. And he said unto him, I am the Lord that brought thee out of Ur of the Chaldees, to give thee this **land** to inherit it.*" "*In the same day the Lord made a covenant with Abram, saying, **Unto thy seed** have I given this land, from the river of Egypt unto the great river, the river Euphrates:*" **Genesis 15:5-7,18**

*"And I will establish my covenant between me and thee and thy seed after thee in their generations for an everlasting covenant, to be a God unto thee, and to thy **seed** after thee. And I will give unto thee, and to thy **seed** after thee, the land wherein thou art a stranger, all the land of Canaan, for an everlasting possession; and I will be their God."* **Genesis 17:7-8**

*"That in blessing I will bless thee, and in multiplying I will multiply thy **seed** as the stars of the heaven, and as the sand which is upon the sea shore; and thy **seed** shall possess the gate of his enemies; And in thy **seed** shall all the nations of the earth be blessed; because thou hast obeyed my voice."* **Genesis 22:17,18**

Abraham believed in the blessing and the Promised *Seed* and was accounted righteous.   **John 8:56**

5. **Read Galatians 3:16 :** Who was Abraham's seed?

God tells Abraham,

1. There is a land where I would like you to go to.

2. You and your children will live here forever.

3. Through your *seed* the whole earth will be blessed.

4. You will have a *seed* who will include many people.

5. Your *seed* will become as many as the stars in the sky.

    [This suggests that he would have many spiritual (*stars in heaven*) as well natural (as *"the dust of the earth"*) descendants.]

6. Your *seed* will enjoy a personal relationship with God.

7. Your *seed* will have victory against your enemies.

8. The **land** promised to you is the inheritance of the entire world.

Hebrews 11:13 reminds us that Abraham did not receive the promises in his lifetime.

"These all died in faith, not having received the promises, but having seen them afar off, and were persuaded of them, and embraced them, and confessed that they were strangers and pilgrims on the earth."

The goal of Abraham's Covenant is that **all** the families of the earth will inherit **all** the earth and experience **all** the blessings of God's presence in the Kingdom. God keeps His promises. There will come a day when Abraham and **all** who have those promises made to them will receive them in full.

6. **Read Genesis 26:1-6; Genesis 35:9-12** : Do you see the continuation of the promise to the seed?

7. **Read Genesis 49:8-12 :** This prophecy is about the Messiah. Which tribe would He come from?

So, the goal of the Abraham's covenant was the same as the original goal of all creation. This purpose is further unfolded in the covenants made to Moses, David and prophesied by Jeremiah.

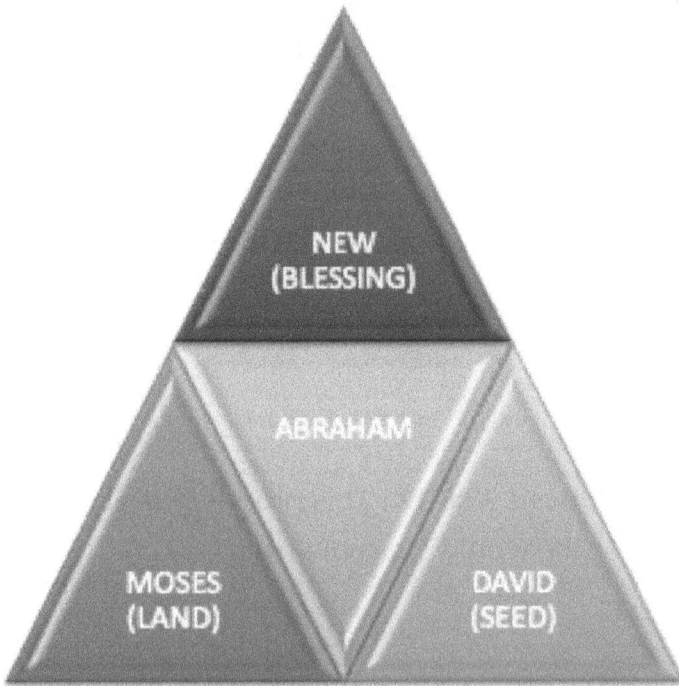

A **Land** that extends to the corners of the earth,

A **Seed** that includes all the families of the earth,

& the **Blessing** of God's presence.

Abraham's covenant is the promise of God's Kingdom in all the earth, for all the peoples of the earth.

Abraham's covenant is unconditional.

Genesis 15

But, God will not bless an unrighteous and sinful nation. **Genesis 17:1-2; 18:17-19; 22:15-18; 26:2-5**

So God creates a *"chosen generation, a royal priesthood, a holy nation, a peculiar people"* **1 Peter 2:9**

Week 11: The Land (Moses' Covenant)

In **Exodus 2:24** we are told God heard the groaning of His people *"and God remembered his covenant with Abraham, with Isaac, and with Jacob. And God looked upon the children of Israel, and God had respect unto them."*

In **Exodus 6:6-8**, God tells Israel *" I will bring you out from under the burdens of the Egyptians, and I will rid you out of their bondage, and I will redeem you with a stretched out arm, and with great judgments: And I will take you to me for a people, and I will be to you a God: and ye shall know that I am the Lord your God, which bringeth you out from under the burdens of the Egyptians. And I will bring you in unto the land, concerning the which I did swear to give it to Abraham, to Isaac, and to Jacob; and I will give it you for an heritage: I am the Lord."*

He remembers the promise he made to Abraham and to the children of Israel, who are Abraham's seed. This is simply God keeping His Word to Abraham.

1. **Read Exodus 23:31-33** : Why were the current people of the land not to live among the Israelites?

2. **Read Exodus 24:1-12 :** What does God say He will give Moses when he comes up into the mount?

By giving Moses the Law, God begins the work of making the *seed* righteous. It was through the Law that God expressed His Will for and to Israel. He reveals to them in the Law how to practically apply their faith in Him and live righteous in His sight.

Moses' Covenant was conditional.

It promised blessings including possession of the land *if* they obeyed. It also warned of curses *if* they disobeyed. **Deuteronomy 27-28**

3. **Read Exodus 6:2-8 :** Does God's covenant with Moses have anything to do with His covenant with Abraham?

God's promises Abraham a **land**, a **seed**, a **blessing**, and a **relationship** with Him. These are the same promises that are at the heart of the covenant that is revealed to Moses.

4. **Read Galatians 3:15-17** : Does the Law replace the covenant with Abraham?

The Law pointed out where Israel fell short.   It could not empower them to obey the Law.   However, the righteous **requirements** of the Law had to be fulfilled in order for God's kingdom to be established on earth.   But who could possibly live free from sin and fulfill the requirements of the Law?

Week 12: The Seed (David's Covenant)

The covenant that God made with the "house of David" is a further unfolding of the promise God made to Abraham. The covenant God made with David promised him an heir to his throne, a *Great King* who would reign over God's great Kingdom forever. In **Psalm 72:17**, Solomon writes that *"men shall be blessed in him: All nations shall call him blessed."*

God promised Abraham that, *"in thee shall all families of the earth be blessed."* This is fulfilled through the life and reign of the coming King, Christ Jesus, who is the seed of Abraham.

Read Luke 1:67-73

1. What *"oath"* did Zechariah see soon being fulfilled?

"Now therefore so shalt thou say unto my servant David, Thus saith the Lord of hosts, I took thee from the sheepcote, from following the sheep, to be ruler over my people, over Israel: And I was with thee whithersoever thou wentest, and have cut off all thine enemies out of thy sight, and have made thee a great name, like unto the name of the great men that are in the earth. Moreover I will appoint a place for my people Israel, and will plant them, that they may dwell in a place of their own, and move no more; neither shall the children of wickedness afflict them any more, as beforetime, And as since the time that I commanded judges to be over my people Israel, and have caused thee to rest from all thine enemies. Also the Lord telleth thee that he will make thee an house.

And when thy days be fulfilled, and thou shalt sleep with thy fathers, **I will set up thy seed after thee**, *which shall proceed out of thy bowels, and I will establish his* **kingdom**. *He shall build an* **house** *for my name, and I will stablish the* **throne** *of his kingdom for ever. I will be his father, and he shall be my son. If he commit iniquity, I will chasten him with the rod of men, and with the stripes of the children of men: But my mercy shall not depart away from him, as I took it from Saul, whom I put away before thee. And thine* **house** *and thy* **kingdom** *shall be established for ever before thee: thy* **throne** *shall be established for ever. According to all these words, and according to all this vision, so did Nathan speak unto David."*

2 Samuel 7:8–17

Read 1 Samuel 8:1-9

2. After over 300 years in the land, what was Israel demanding?

3. Who were they rejecting?

Read Deuteronomy 17:14-20

4. List God's expectations of the king who would rule over His people?

The kings of Israel were meant to be covenant mediators leading Israel by faithfulness to God and to the covenant. But ultimately the kings of Israel failed. To fulfill the Law, a new King of Israel who would have to come to mediate a New Covenant for God's people.

Read 2 Samuel 7:1-29 & Psalm 89

5. What promises did God make to David?

Malkhut Beit David **מלכות בית דוד** is Hebrew for the "Royal House of David". It refers to David's blood line and David's seed. Those who are directly related to him which, God says, *"shall proceed out of thy bowels."* To be the next king and sit on David's throne you had to be born into the "house" of David.

In **2 Samuel 7:4-29** and **Psalms 89** we see God promises to establish the **seed, throne** and **kingdom** of David, over Israel, and over the whole earth.

Read Zechariah 12:8

6. What else did God promise the house of David?

"Behold, the days come, saith the Lord, that I will raise unto David a righteous Branch, and a King shall reign and prosper, and shall execute judgment and justice in the earth.   In his days Judah shall be saved, and Israel shall dwell safely: and this is his name whereby he shall be called, THE LORD OUR RIGHTEOUSNESS"
Jeremiah 23:5–6

7. What picture of the "**Kingdom of God**" do you see emerging in the Old Testament?

8. **Read Luke 1:31-33 :** What did the angel tell Mary?

9. **Read Matthew 24:14 :** What must happen before the end?

10. **Read 1 Corinthians 15:20-25 :** What happens when *"cometh the end"*?

God promised to give the *Seed* the throne of David in Jerusalem. He would establish His Kingdom so that man will again be ruling over the earth with the promised *Seed* as their King forever. Christ is the *"Seed," "Heir,"* and *"King"* promised to David.

The second Adam will restore what, through sin, the first Adam lost. This is the purpose of the promised *Seed* and the reason for the promise.

He would be born in Bethlehem (**Micah 5:2**) and the offspring of David (**2 Samuel 7:12-16**). God would establish the *Seed* through David, promising him *"And thine **house** and thy Kingdom shall be established for ever before thee: thy throne shall be established for ever."* **2 Samuel 7:16**

Week 13: The Blessing (New Covenant)

Jeremiah 31:31-34: *"Behold, the days come, saith the Lord, That I will make a new covenant With the house of Israel, and with the house of Judah: Not according to the covenant that I made with their fathers In the day that I took them by the hand To bring them out of the land of Egypt; Which my covenant they brake, Although I was an husband unto them, saith the Lord: But this shall be the covenant that I will make with the house of Israel; After those days, saith the Lord,*

> *I will put my law in their inward parts,*
>
> *And write it in their hearts;*
>
> *And will be their God,*
>
> *And they shall be my people.*

And they shall teach no more every man his neighbour, and every man his brother, saying,

> *Know the Lord:*
>
> *For they shall all know me,*
>
> *From the least of them unto the greatest of them,*
>
> *saith the Lord:*
>
> *For I will forgive their iniquity,*
>
> *And I will remember their sin no more."*

Joel 2:28-32

"And it shall come to pass afterward, That I will **pour out my spirit** *upon all flesh; And your sons and your daughters shall prophesy, Your old men shall dream dreams, Your young men shall see visions: And also upon the servants and upon the handmaids In those days will I* **pour out my spirit**. *And I will shew wonders in the heavens and in the earth, Blood, and fire, and pillars of smoke. The sun shall be turned into darkness, and the moon into blood, Before the great and the terrible day of the Lord come. And it shall come to pass, that whosoever shall call on the name of the Lord shall be delivered: For in mount Zion and in Jerusalem shall be deliverance, As the Lord hath said, And in the remnant whom the Lord shall call."*

God promised a New Covenant that would revive, redeem and restore the **seed**. It would **empower** the **seed** to live righteously through the out pouring of His Spirit. God promised that when this New Covenant came, the requirements of the Law would be perfectly fulfilled in the **seed**. The New Covenant would finally fulfill God's promise to Abraham and the **seed** would endure and possess the **land** forever.

Read Jeremiah 11:1-11

1. What Covenant had Israel and Judah broken?

2. How did they *"walk"*? What would God do about it?

3. **Read Hebrews 7-13; 9:13-15 :** Who would be the mediator of this New Covenant?

4. **Read Isaiah 42:5-7; 55:1-5 :** Was it just to the house of Israel and the house of Judah, or was it to all the nations?

5. **Read Romans 3:24-31 :** Who would qualify to be *"covered"* under the New Covenant?

6. **Read John 10:11-16** : What does Jesus mean when He says He has sheep *"not of this fold"*?

Read Ephesians 2:11-19

7. According to Paul, what are we?

8. What are we heirs of? Why?

The New Covenant of **Matthew 26:26-29; Hebrews 8-9;** and **Jeremiah 31:31-34** rests upon the sacrifice of Christ. It secures the blessings promised to Abraham for all believers. **Galatians 3:13-29**

It is absolutely unconditional. There is no responsibility on our part. It is final and irreversible. The blood of Christ is its foundation. **Matthew 26:28; 1 Corinthians 11:25**

God had all this in view when he made a covenant with Abraham. He saw the winning of the nations of the world to Christ. He saw the gathering of the saints to that heavenly city. This is what God was promising Abraham. The rest of the Bible is simply shows the outworking of that promise.

Abraham and his descendants understood that God's covenant was not about a piece of real estate. It was about reviving and redeeming a people and restoring a Kingdom. It was about a *Seed* in which every promise would be fulfilled. Someone, in whom *"all the promises of God are yes!"*

WEEK 14: "ALL THE PROMISES OF GOD IN HIM ARE YES!"

"Forasmuch as ye know that ye were not redeemed with corruptible things, as silver and gold, from your vain conversation received by tradition from your fathers;

But with the precious blood of Christ, as of a lamb without blemish and without spot:

Who verily was foreordained before the foundation of the world, but was manifest in these last times for you," **1 Peter 1:18-20**

The promised *Seed* would be the perfect King, descended from David and would sit on His father David's throne. **Psalms 2; 2 Samuel 7:12-16**

"Behold, the days come, saith the LORD, that I will raise unto David a righteous Branch, and a King shall reign and prosper, and shall execute judgment and justice in the earth." **Jeremiah 23:5**

The promised *Seed* is Israel's *promised* King.   He is the "*Messiah*", a Hebrew term referring to the Lord's *Anointed One*.   The one who in the New Testament is called *"Messiah"* or *"Christ"*.

"Jesus": is Greek for the Hebrew *"Jeshua"* or Joshua, meaning *"the Lord is salvation."*

"Christ": from the Greek *"Christos"* for the Hebrew *"Mashiah,"* meaning **"anointed."**

"Messiah": from the Greek *"Messias"* for the Hebrew *"Mashiah,"* meaning *"Anointed One."*

Jesus *(Savior)* **+** Christ *(Anointed One)* =

The *Anointed Savior*

Prophets, priests, and kings were anointed with oil to set them apart and empower them for service to God.   A king was designated by the out pouring of oil over his head.   This act was called being *anointed*.   The oil represents the Holy Spirit.   This is the origin of the term '*Messiah*'.

In **John 1:32,33; Luke 4:18,** Jesus was personally *anointed* by the Holy Spirit himself.

He taught that:

1. God will establish His **direct** rule or government in the earth through His Son. **Psalms 2**

2. God will establish peace and judge the earth with righteousness. **Psalms 98:9**

3. God will hold every man accountable for the deeds of this life. **Ezekiel 18:4**

4. God will *restore* all things. **Acts 3:21**

5. God will *remove* every curse. **Revelation 22:3**

6. The Son of man will return in the Glory of God. **Matthew 16:27**

7. When the Son of man returns, God's Glory will reside in Jerusalem. **Isaiah 4:5**

8. Every form of human government will be abolished. Every constitution will be voided because the government will *"rest on His shoulders."* **Isaiah 9:6**

9. *" That at the name of Jesus every knee should bow, of things in heaven, and things in earth, and things under the earth; And that every tongue should confess that Jesus Christ is Lord, to the glory of God the Father."* **Philippians 2:10-11**

1. **Read Daniel 7:13-14 :** What is given to the *"one like the son of man"* by the *"Ancient of Days"*?

2. **Read Revelation 1:1-18 :** How does John's description of Jesus compare with Daniel's vision?

Jesus taught us to pray: *"Thy **Kingdom** come, Thy will be done in earth, as it is in heaven."* **Matthew 6:10**

It is this Kingdom which will be established by the *Seed* on earth when He returns.   Just as God's Will is obeyed, without question, by the angels in heaven (**Psalm 103:19-21**), so it will be throughout all the earth.

The body of Christ is made up of Abraham's seed, Jews and Gentiles in one body, who can now look to inherit the **land** as citizens of God's coming *Kingdom* on earth.

3. **Read Hebrews 11:39-40; 12:22-24,28 :** As a believer, what is your inheritance?

To inherit this heavenly city, country and Kingdom is to inherit all the earth as the chosen seed of Abraham. **Matthew 5:3,5**

4. **Read 2 Peter 3:13 & Revelation 21:1-4 :** What is it saying?

Read Revelation 22:12-21

5. How does Jesus' second coming fulfill the prophecies about the Kingdom of God?

6. What is the significance of the Tree of Life and Jesus being the offspring of David?

Read Hebrews 9:1-28

7. Was Jesus qualified to be the mediator of a new covenant?

8. Why?

Read Matthew 1:1

9. Was Jesus the Son of David?

10. Was Jesus a descendent of Abraham?

Remember, to **sin** is to *"transgress"* or act in opposition to the Will of God. It was through the Law that God expressed His Will for His people. To fulfill the Law, you must keep the **whole** Law.

"For whosoever shall keep the whole law, and yet offend in one point, he is guilty of all." **James 2:10**

Read Matthew 5:17-20; 1 John 3:4-5

11. Did Jesus fulfill the requirements of the Law of Moses?

12. How? **Hebrews 4:15; 7:26; 1 Peter 2:22; 1 John 3:5**

Read Galatians 3:13

13. What Did Jesus suffer?

14. How?

CONCLUSION

God revealed His purpose to us in His covenant.   God is fulfilling His purposes through Christ.   Every promise and purpose of God is revealed and fulfilled in Christ Jesus.   *"For all the promises of God in Him are yea, ..."* **2 Corinthians 1:20**

God *" hath made him to be sin for us, who knew no sin; that we might be made the righteousness of God in him."* **2 Corinthians 5:21**

God revealed His covenant...

In Eden - Genesis 1:26-30, establishes His Kingdom and His purpose.   Adam, the first man failed.   But Christ, as the "second Man," the "last Adam" (**1 Corinthians 15:45-47**) will reign over all the things which the first Adam lost. **Colossians 2:10; Hebrews 2:7-8**

To Adam - Genesis 3, establishes the conditions for life after the fall but promises a Redeemer.   Christ is the *"Seed of the woman"* who will crush the serpent's head. The One promised to Adam. **Genesis 3:15; John 12:31; 1 John 3:8; Galatians 4:4-5**

To Abraham - Genesis 12:1-3; 15; 17; 22, establishes the nation of Israel and confirms God's promise to revive, redeem and restore His people and His Kingdom.   Jesus is the *"Seed to whom the promises were made."* **Genesis 22:18; Galatians 3:16**

To Moses (*the Land*) - Exodus 20-40; Deuteronomy 27-30; The Law condemns all men, *"for that all have sinned."*   But Christ lived sinlessly under the Law and bore for us the curse of the Law.   **Galatians 3:10-14**

To David (*the Seed*) - II Samuel 7:4-29; Psalms 89, establishes the seed, throne and kingdom of David, over Israel, and over the whole earth.   Christ is the *"Seed," "Heir,"* and *"King"* promised to David.

The Blessing (*New Covenant*) - Matthew 26:26-29; Hebrews 8-9; Jeremiah 31:31-34, rests upon the sacrifice of Christ.   It secures the blessings promised to Abraham for all believers. **Galatians 3:13-29**

It is absolutely unconditional with no responsibility on our part.   It is final and irreversible.   The blood of Christ is its foundation.   **Matthew 26:28; 1 Corinthians 11:25**

In **Revelation 13:8**, Jesus is called, *"the Lamb slain from the foundation of the world."*

This should tell the reader four things:

1. God has a plan.

2. God does not make mistakes.

3. God made provision before the problem.

4. The benefits of Christ's sacrifice are available for everyone who believes.

That means Old testament saints that looked forward to the promise are washed clean in Christ's blood just the same as we are today, just as if the sacrifice had been made before the foundation of the world.

To implement His plan and sustain His purpose, God made a promise with Himself for our preservation.   **Hebrews 13:20-21; Isaiah 55:3**

The covenants show how He progressively revealed His eternal purpose to us. Abraham's seed will live forever in the new earth and the New Jerusalem. The Kingdom of God will be established on this earth forever, and ever, and ever. **Revelations 21-22**

God is determined to give us eternal life and fellowship with Him, in spite of our unworthiness.   This is still God's promise to any person who turns to Him in repentance and faith.   Christ's death serves as the oath, pledge and promise God made to us.   *"For God so loved the world, that he gave his only begotten Son, that whosoever believeth in him should not perish, but have everlasting life."* **John 3:16**

"But now is Christ risen from the dead, and become the firstfruits of them that slept.   For since by man came death, by man came also the resurrection of the dead.   For as in Adam all die, even so in Christ shall all be made alive.   But every man in his own order: Christ the firstfruits; afterward they that are Christ's at his coming.   Then cometh the end, when he shall have delivered up the kingdom to God, even the Father; when he shall have put down all rule and all authority and power.   For he must reign, till he hath put all enemies under his feet.   The last enemy that shall be destroyed is death.   For he hath put all things under his feet.   But when he saith, all things are put under him, it is manifest that he is excepted, which did put all things under him.   And when all things shall be subdued unto him, then shall the Son also himself be subject unto him that put all things under him, that God may be all in all."

1 Corinthians 15:20-28

Know, *"That if thou shalt confess with thy mouth the Lord Jesus, and shalt believe in thine heart that God hath raised him from the dead, thou shalt be saved. For with the heart man believeth unto righteousness; and with the mouth confession is made unto salvation. For the scripture saith, Whosoever believeth on him shall not be ashamed. For there is no difference between the Jew and the Greek: for the same Lord over all is rich unto all that call upon him. For whosoever shall call upon the name of the Lord shall be saved."* **Romans 10:9-13**

Jesus Christ is still Lord, King and Sovereign, whether you acknowledge Him or not. He alone is worthy. We accept Him as our *Savio*r when we confess and acknowledge Him for who He is, and we accept in our heart what He has done to bring about that salvation.

Is He your Lord *and* Savior? Have you asked Him to come into your life? Have you allowed Him to rule *over* your life? If not, I encourage you to call on His name now. There is salvation and deliverance in that Name.

About the Author

Elder Dorian G. Newton, a native of Houston, Texas, grew up in the church and on July 1, 1990, after answering the call to the ministry, he was licensed to preach the Gospel. Shortly after high school he enlisted in the United States Navy and remained on active duty until 2002, during which time he met his wife, the lovely Jermaine Newton.

He is a graduate of Old Dominion University and is currently pursuing his Master's degree at George Washington University. In 2007, he became a covenant partner with Tabernacle of Prayer Church (T.O.P.C.) serving under his pastor, Dr. Minnie B. Washington.   On December 13, 2009, under presiding Bishop Spencer H. Riddick, Jr., he was officially ordained and recognized as an Elder of Tabernacle of Prayer Church.

Elder Newton has served in a variety of capacities during his time with T.O.P.C. and is the current Director of the Men's Ministry, the Freedom in Redemption Evangelism Ministry (*F.IR.E.*) and conducts weekly Bible study classes.   Most importantly, he is a preacher, a teacher and a true servant of God who is filled with the Holy Ghost and stands daily on his favorite scripture, Romans 8:28 which reads, *" And we know that all things work together for good to them that love God, to them who are the called according to his purpose."*

IN THE RIGHT HANDS, THIS BOOK WILL CHANGE LIVES!

MOST PEOPLE WHO NEED THIS MESSAGE WILL NOT BE LOOKING FOR THIS BOOK. PUT A COPY OF THIS BOOK INTO THEIR HANDS.

"NOW THE PARABLE IS THIS: THE SEED IS THE WORD OF GOD. BUT THAT ON THE GOOD GROUND ARE THEY, WHICH IN AN HONEST AND GOOD HEART, HAVING HEARD THE WORD, KEEP IT, AND BRING FORTH FRUIT WITH PATIENCE.

NO MAN, WHEN HE HATH LIGHTED A CANDLE, COVERETH IT WITH A VESSEL, OR PUTTETH IT UNDER A BED; BUT SETTETH IT ON A CANDLESTICK, THAT THEY WHICH ENTER IN MAY SEE THE LIGHT."
LUKE 8: 11, 15-16.

OUR MINISTRY IS CONSTANTLY SEEKING METHODS TO FIND THE "GOOD GROUND" & PEOPLE WHOSE LIVES NEED CHANGING. THEY ARE WAITING IN THE PRISONS, ON THE STREET CORNERS, OR EVEN IN YOUR HOME. BLESS SOMEONE, TODAY.

EXTEND THIS MINISTRY BY SOWING
3 BOOKS, 5 BOOKS, 10 BOOKS, OR MORE TODAY!

A Monthly Christian Newsletter — Issue No 1 - September 1, 2011

Know Christ Today.org

"But what things were gain to me, those I counted loss for Christ...that I may know him, and the power of his resurrection, and the fellowship of his sufferings, ..." -- Philippians 3: 7,10

A teaching Web-Ministry founded " for the perfecting of the saints, for the work of the ministry, for the edifying of the body of Christ..." "That we henceforth be no more children, tossed to and fro, and carried about with every wind of doctrine, by the sleight of men, and cunning craftiness, whereby they lie in wait to deceive; but speaking the truth in love, may grow up into him in all things, which is the head, even Christ." --Ephesians 4:12, 14-15

United Men's Fellowship Breakfast 2nd Quarter	What are the Three Tenses of Salvation?	What is the Gospel and why is it "good news"?	CALENDAR OF EVENTS

United Men's Fellowship Breakfast 2nd Quarter
July 9, 2011
Speaker: Elder J. Wilmer, Sr.
Tabernacle of Prayer Church
Title: **Men of God**
Scripture: Joshua 24:5
Proverbs 22:6 Ephesians 5:25, 28
Main Point: God has chosen men to be the "Head of the family"
Page 2

What are the Three Tenses of Salvation?
God "saves" us in three tenses - past, present, & future. This means you have been saved from the penalty of sin; you are being saved from the power of sin; you shall be saved from the presence of sin.
Page 3

What is the Gospel and why is it "good news"?
In Romans 1:16, Paul says he is not ashamed of the gospel or "good news" of Christ, because it has the power to save those who believe it. But then what exactly was the "good news" that Paul was preaching?
Page 4

CALENDAR OF EVENTS
Page 2

BIBLE TRIVIA
Page 2

SEPTEMBER PRAYER FOCUS & READING PLAN
Page 3

Know Christ Today.org website launched September 1st

"But what things were gain to me, those I counted loss for Christ...that I may know him, and the power of his resurrection, and the fellowship of his sufferings, ..." -- Philippians 3: 7,10

Know Christ Today.org is a teaching Web-Ministry founded by Christ through Elder Dorian G. Newton " for the perfecting of the saints, for the work of the ministry, for the edifying of the body of Christ..." "That we henceforth be no more children, tossed to and fro, and carried about with every wind of doctrine, by the sleight of men, and cunning craftiness, whereby they lie in wait to deceive; but speaking the truth in love, may grow up into him in all things, which is the head, even Christ." -Ephesians 4:12, 14-15.

The website will act as a hub to provide leadership training, podcasts of sermons and lectures, various training and teaching ministries, a monthly e-newsletter, bible study instruction and resource materials, access to published materials produced by the ministry and a calendar of local events and activities.

Other ministries found on the website are:

Freedom in Redemption Evangelism (F.I.R.E.) Ministry is an ongoing dynamic inductive Bible study started by Deacon Gilbert Hernandez in 2007. We focus on evangelism, interpretation and application of God's Word. We meet 7:30 p.m every Friday Night for an hour long study at *Tabernacle of Prayer Church, 315 S. Rosemont Rd., Virginia Beach, VA 23451.*

United Men's Fellowship Ministry, founded in 2007 by Minister Steve Siplin, is inclusive of all men. This "Ground Breaking" ministry seeks to dissolve negative habits and stereotypical behaviors. It sponsors a quarterly prayer breakfast, men's conferences, annual Men's Day, and addresses men's issues.

We meet at 8:00 a.m. for a 2 hour men's prayer breakfast on the 2nd Saturday of each quarter at the *Golden Corral located at 1436 Kempsville Road, Virginia Beach - (757) 467-3424.*

Please visit the website for contact information and sign up for the newsletter, use the studies, and come out to the fellowships.
